400 KILOMETRES

400 KILOMETRES

Drew Hayden Taylor

Talonbooks
Vancouver

Talonbooks
P.O. Box 2076, Vancouver, British Columbia, Canada V6B 3S3
www.talonbooks.com

Typeset in New Baskerville and printed and bound in Canada.

Second Printing: February 2008

The publisher gratefully acknowledges the financial support of the
Canada Council for the Arts; the Government of Canada through the
Book Publishing Industry Development Program; and the Province of
British Columbia through the British Columbia Arts Council for our
publishing activities.

Library and Archives Canada Cataloguing in Publication

Taylor, Drew Hayden, 1962–
    400 kilometres / Drew Hayden Taylor.

A play.
ISBN 0-88922-517-6

    I. Title. II. Title: Four hundred kilometres.

PS8589.A885F69 2005   C812'.54   C2004-906434-7

ISBN-13: 978-0-88922-517-6

INTRODUCTION

400 kilometres ... it almost seems that I've travelled that far on foot since I started the story of Janice Wirth and the Wabung family all those years ago. An Ojibway word, Wabung translates into English as "tomorrow," and there certainly has been a lot of tomorrows since I started the *Someday* trilogy back in 1991. But before I continue my own story, I must acknowledge the life of a man who was largely responsible for my success in Native theatre; who directed and dramaturged the original story; and who has now moved on to the next world ... the irreplaceable Larry Lewis. Yet he lives on in all these stories.

What began so long ago as a simple way of exploring the repercussions the "scoop-up" (the colonial practice of removing infants from their birth mothers on Indian reserves and adopting them out to white families "for their own good") had on Native families has almost turned into a little cottage industry itself. And no one more than I was surprised at the success of *Someday* and *Only Drunks and Children Tell the Truth.* In fact, one woman after seeing *Only Drunks* ... several times, sent a fan letter to both me and the character Tonto. She even urged me to write a one-man show around him. That was definitely a first for me. And maybe, "someday," I will do it.

When I wrote *Someday*, first as a short story, then as a play, I had absolutely no intention of making it into a trilogy. My imagination did not extend that far. But after Janice walks out the Wabung family door at the end of *Someday* and presumably out of her birth family's life, I was pestered with questions about how appropriate that ending was, or even if it was an ending at all. Some were afraid it implied that there was little chance of children that had been adopted out ever reconciling with their birth families. I definitely felt the onus to further explore that reality. Thus was born *Only Drunks and Children Tell the Truth*—more a story about Janice's personal journey than *Someday*'s Wabung family drama.

At the end of *Only Drunks* ... I felt I had left the audience with a stronger sense of completion, or at the very least, an implied closure to Janice's story. It had ended on a more positive note. But again, I felt the story hadn't been fully completed. As with the tragic stories of residential schools and other such horrific government policies imposed on Native peoples, the after-effects are often generational in reach—the ingrained dysfunction can often be passed on. Part of the Seventh Generation prophecy is that every decision you make will have repercussions seven generations down the road, so you should always take that into consideration and have it guide your actions. So what about the generation after Janice ... what would the effect of the "scoop-up" be on them?

From that question came *400 Kilometres*, the distance between both of Janice's homes in Otter Lake and in London, Ontario. I'm told it's a metaphor thing. Janice, now pregnant, is awash in confusion ... and let me tell you, writing a story from the perspective of a pregnant woman was a real test of abilities for this particular writer.

Actresses who have played Janice in many of the play's productions have told me that often after the performances, there were usually one or two Native people, usually women, waiting for the actress to come out of the change room at the end of the show, telling her: "That is my story." And though emotionally and physically exhausted from doing the two-hour show, the actresses usually found the time to sit down and talk with these individuals, helping them on their cathartic journey. I felt the same way about my beloved Janice. Every couple of years she wanted to talk, and what kind of friend would I have been if I hadn't listened?

The story started with a family wondering what had happened to a little child the government took away 35 years ago—a mother wondering about her daughter. As things often happen in the Native community, the story has come full circle, and now it's time for Janice to deal with motherhood, and all the wondering that entails.

The story is now closed. Janice has found her niche in the world. Hers is about 400 kilometres long.

Drew Hayden Taylor
December 2004
Toronto, Ontario

400 Kilometres was first produced by Two Planks and a Passion Theatre on March 19, 1999 in Wolfville, Nova Scotia as part of the Atlantic Theatre Festival, with the following cast and crew:

JANICE/GRACE	Shalan Joudry
TONTO	Kennetch Charlette
LLOYD	John Dartt
THERESA	Jean Morpurgo
ANNE	Pam Matthews

Directed by Ken Schwartz
Set design by Ian Pygott
Costumes by Aetna Gallagher
Original music by Jeff Hennessy

ACT ONE

Scene One

*Lights up on ANNE WABUNG, an elderly Native
woman sitting somewhere in the theatre, a fair
distance from much younger JANICE
WIRTH/GRACE WABUNG who is sitting on the
dark stage. ANNE is talking while sewing white
baby clothes, her voice searching out and finding
JANICE/GRACE. She exudes a warm, motherly
personality which JANICE is drawn to. JANICE does
not move, nor speak but ANNE has her full
attention.*

ANNE

Did I ever tell you where the name Otter Lake
came from? No? Well, then I should tell you. It's
important that you know about the place you
come from. Now, as my grandfather tells it, and
keep in mind this isn't necessarily gospel. If the
story wasn't interesting enough, my grandfather
was known to add a few details here and there to
make it really interesting. It seems that a long
time ago, the Chuganosh … that's what we called

white people, were still trying to figure this land out. These fur traders came paddling their way up Otter Lake one day. In this one particular canoe were a bunch of scruffy Frenchmen and a Jesuit. They were looking to build a settlement of some kind to trade for furs with the Annishnawbe. That's us. And much like Columbus, the Chuganosh were lost. Somewhere along the way, they took the wrong river or lake, the one they were looking for was a couple miles up stream. But the Jesuit was sure they were in the right lake and started to give orders about setting up camp, but the French guide started arguing with him. He knew they were in the wrong place. They were supposed to be in the other lake. He kept trying to tell that to the Jesuit who refused to listen. "No, no," the guide kept saying in his thick French accent, "that is de ot'er lake. De ot'er lake." That is why we are known as the Otter Lake Band of the Great Ojibway Nation. It only goes to show, Grace, that regardless of where the name comes from, it can still be a place to be proud of.

Scene Two

Lights up on the home of LLOYD and THERESA WIRTH, a well-to-do older non-Native couple enjoying their retirement. The house, in particular the living room, is tastefully and expensively decorated with knick-knacks from around the world. THERESA enters the room and checks herself in the mirror. She is dressed for an evening out.

THERESA

Darling, did I leave my earrings on the dresser?

There is silence.

Darling?

Annoyed, she opens a small drawer, rustles around and pulls out a small device.

I swear, that man …

She exits, still muttering. There is a pause, then she enters again, putting her earrings in.

Keep your hearing aid in. I hate talking to myself.

She is followed by LLOYD WIRTH, a mature man also set for an evening out.

LLOYD

Why? Keeps the plants healthy.

THERESA
I'm serious Lloyd, you've already lost three of
those since you got them.

LLOYD
Yes dear. You look splendid.

THERESA
I look fat.

LLOYD
I like women with a little meat on them.

THERESA gives him a stern look.

Then again, maybe I don't.

THERESA
At my age, maybe I should stop wearing dresses
that are so tight. What do you think?

LLOYD
It's questions like this that make me lose my
hearing aids. Wear whatever you want. Are you
ready yet?

THERESA
Almost.

LLOYD
Translation: at least another 20 minutes.

THERESA
Done. Now the question is, are you ready?

LLOYD
For the last quarter hour.

THERESA
Where are the car keys?

LLOYD reaches into his pocket only to come up with empty hands.

LLOYD
I hate you.

THERESA
You did make the reservations, didn't you?

LLOYD
Of course.

THERESA
Not that I don't trust you, darling, but maybe I should phone just to check on them ...

LLOYD
Don't you dare. I made them. Please grant me some respect in our declining years.

THERESA
Just wanting to make sure, darling. We'd better hurry if we want to fit dinner in before the show. Let's see, answering machine is on, turn on the alarm ...

LLOYD
Do you realize this thing costs more than what it's supposed to protect?

THERESA is getting her coat out of the closet but stops moving. She glances across the house, her eyes taking in the memories.

LLOYD

Theresa? Are you alright? You don't look ...

THERESA

Yes, I'm quite alright. It just hit me that we're really going to go through with it.

LLOYD

Don't tell me you're having second thoughts? It's not too late. It was only a suggestion.

THERESA

It was the right one. I know you, Lloyd Wirth. You do not make foolish suggestions. You think things out. It's the only good thing being a lawyer taught you. I'm just being emotional.

LLOYD

Forty-two years in this house. Three children. Four dogs and I don't know how many ferns. That's a lot of memories to walk away from.

THERESA

It will be sad.

LLOYD

If you let it.

THERESA

I like to think of it as a new adventure. Or picking the one up that we left behind.

LLOYD

No adventures please. I have enough trouble
sleeping at nights as it is.

THERESA

You're getting old, Mr. Wirth.

LLOYD

What was your first clue—the thinning hair, the
bad hearing, failing memory, or the plethora of
snaps and pops that happen every time I stretch?

THERESA

It was your crankiness.

LLOYD

Me?

THERESA

You.

LLOYD

I don't know what you mean. But if you want to
talk irritability …

THERESA

The play, darling, the play.

The doorbell rings.

THERESA

Oh bother, what now?

LLOYD

Whoever is at the door, make it quick. I'm
hungry.

THERESA opens the door revealing JANICE WIRTH/GRACE WABUNG.

THERESA
Janice?!

JANICE
Hello mother.

LLOYD
Theresa, who the devil is it?

THERESA
It's Janice, darling. Do come in, dear.

JANICE enters the house.

JANICE
Good evening.

LLOYD
Janice? What are you doing here?

JANICE
Oh, I'm sorry. I should have called.

THERESA
No, no, sit down. It is polite to call ahead but you're always welcome here. You know that.

JANICE
Thank you.

LLOYD
Anything the matter? It's not like you to suddenly show up like this.

JANICE

No, everything's fine. I ... just felt like coming home for a visit. I'm allowed, aren't I?

LLOYD

I bet she had a fight with that boyfriend of hers.

THERESA

Now Lloyd, leave the poor girl alone. She just arrived. There is nothing wrong ...

JANICE

I'm fine. Whatever you two were going to do tonight ... please just go ahead. Maybe I'll just soak in the hot tub or something until you get back. Something wonderfully relaxing like that.

THERESA

I have a fabulous idea. Why don't you come with us? Make it a family outing. Wouldn't that be wonderful, Lloyd?

LLOYD

Theresa! It's opening night! A spare ticket would be imposs ...

THERESA

You're on the board. What is the point of being on a board if you can't pull strings?

JANICE

Daddy, don't worry about it. I'll be fine here.

THERESA
You sure? Lloyd is an old string-puller from way back.

JANICE
What are you going to see?

THERESA
Shaw's *Caesar and Cleopatra.*

LLOYD
Rumour has it, it's supposed to be an excellent production.

JANICE
Then enjoy the play.

THERESA
But you love the theatre.

JANICE
Not tonight.

LLOYD
We'd better get a move on. I don't usually enjoy these radical re-interpretations of the classics. In this one, Caesar is supposed to be a powerful corporate executive and Cleopatra is a thinly veiled Athena Onassis.

JANICE
Who?

THERESA
You should read *People* magazine more.

LLOYD

She's Aristotle Onassis's granddaughter.
Christine's only daughter. She's just a child and is
the sole heir to his shipping empire.

THERESA

Only fifteen billion dollars.

LLOYD

Bit of a theatrical stretch if you ask my opinion.

THERESA

Nobody did, darling.

LLOYD

Damn fool revisionists. Caesar was Caesar and
Cleopatra was Cleopatra.

THERESA

Thus the name. Lloyd, I don't think I'm
interested in going anymore.

JANICE

Oh please Mother, don't stay home on my
account.

THERESA

We don't see nearly enough of you. You
unexpectedly show up on our doorstep, and
assume I'd leave you to see a production of a
show I've seen at least four times? How little you
know me. I'll wait till the fifth production.

LLOYD
> Need I remind you that you are on the
> fundraising committee. You chair the fundraising
> committee.

THERESA
> Lloyd, I don't want to go to the play.

LLOYD
> Not more than five minutes ago you said ...

THERESA
> Don't be annoying, dear.

LLOYD
> What will I tell people?

THERESA
> Whatever you want. Tell them I'm ill.

JANICE
> Maybe I should have stayed home ...

THERESA
> Nonsense. You are home now. Do you still want
> that hot tub or not?

JANICE
> It would be nice.

THERESA
> Wonderful. I'll turn it on for you, nice and hot. I
> just might join you myself.

JANICE

Fabulous. There's nothing quite like a nice hot soak. I need it.

LLOYD

Excuse me. I'm not dead yet. Do I have a say in any of this?

THERESA

Yes darling. Say whatever you want.

LLOYD

Theresa, we do have an official obligation to watch the damn thing. Can we at least see the play tomorrow night?

THERESA

That's fine with me. And maybe by then we might persuade Janice to join us. It's been a long time since the three of us went to the theatre together.

JANICE

I didn't really bring anything with me. It was sort of spur of the moment.

THERESA

Hmmm. Well, you still have some of your old clothes in the spare room. I'm sure you can find a bathing suit or something. But please, not that horrible one you wore on our trip to the Bahamas.

JANICE

Like I could still fit it. I'll go look.

JANICE exits.

LLOYD

    I'd better phone and make our apologies. The
things I do for this family.

THERESA

    Lloyd, do you think something's wrong with
Janice? She doesn't seem quite right.

LLOYD

    Janice?! She's a rock. That's the way we raised
her.

THERESA

    She's been through a lot recently and ...

LLOYD

    Janice is fine. She's a tough girl. It's all in the
Wirth name.

THERESA

    She wasn't born a Wirth, darling.

LLOYD

    True but she'll always be a Wirth to me. It's that
boyfriend of hers I'm worried about. What do we
really know about him?

THERESA

    You're her father. You're supposed to be worried
about her boyfriends. But she is thirty-seven,
Lloyd. Worrying about boyfriends is a little passé
at this point.

LLOYD

It's like tweed. It's never passé.

THERESA

Perhaps you'd care to join us in the hot tub?

LLOYD

That's all I need. To develop more wrinkles. I'll pass. I will simply make my phone calls and think up an excuse for not being there.

THERESA

Try not to be too creative.

LLOYD

It is theatre, Theresa. They expect it.

THERESA exits.

I wonder what Shaw would say about this. Probably something witty and long-winded. But then again, he could afford to be witty and long-winded, he was a bachelor.

He pours himself a scotch.

Scene Three

ANNE appears again. JANICE remains on stage, silently watching.

ANNE

I knew within hours that you were growing inside me, Grace. Your father had been away for ten days hunting deer. When Frank came back, well, let's just say he missed me an awful lot. Almost too much. When I woke up that next morning, I just knew you were somewhere inside me. Don't ask me why. I've heard that there's no logical way a woman would know or could tell. So them doctors say. But have you ever noticed them doctors are usually men? So how would they know? But I didn't tell your father. Not just yet. We'd only been married about eight months or so and we were still fitting into married life. And I wanted to make sure. Really sure. I was sure but I wanted to be really really sure, if you know what I mean. So two months passed, and I was really really sure. One morning over breakfast … I still remember what I made that morning. Pancakes with store-bought maple syrup. That was your father's favourite. We had a cousin that made some locally but it always seemed so much fancier back then to buy it from a store. That way you didn't seem so poor. I wanted to put him in a good mood 'cause sometimes with men, you just never know how they're gonna act sometimes. I've seen men react to the news they were going to be fathers like it was just another mouth to feed. Others react like it was the second coming of Christ. So I was a little nervous. I remember his fork was half-way to his mouth when I blurted it out. "Frank," I said, "I'm going to have a baby." Except I said it in Indian. "Frank, nwiibebiisim." For some reason it sounds better in Indian. Anyway, Frank's fork stopped in mid-air. It sort of hung there, syrup dripping off it onto his new, clean pants. I was so nervous. I couldn't tell what he was thinking. Then he calmly put the fork down, looked at me, and smiled. That was all. A big smile. Lots of teeth. His eyes crinkled up just like so. Standing up, he pushed his plate clear across the table which was uncommon for Frank. He always cleaned his plate no matter what I made for him. He tucked in his shirt, kissed me and opened the door to leave. I asked him where he was going. He said so proudly "I've got some bragging to do!" Then it sort of dawned on me, what does he have to be proud of? I was the one that was going to be doing all the work?!

Scene Four

The lights come up on JANICE, in very casual clothing, watching television. She is absent-mindedly flipping through the channels. Sitting at a nearby table, her mother is watching her.

THERESA
Anything good on?

JANICE
Not really.

THERESA
Dear, that's the Latin station.

JANICE
Bueno.

THERESA
Your body is here but your mind is somewhere far away.

JANICE turns the television off.

JANICE
I assure you I am quite here. So, Mother, what is the big secret?

THERESA
I was going to ask you the same question.

JANICE
I beat you to it. I've seen the conspiring looks between you and Father. You two are up to

something, and I have the feeling I arrived just in the middle of it. What have you two got up your sleeves?

THERESA

When did you get so smart?

JANICE

As a child when I figured out that you and Father didn't lock your bedroom door at nights to just keep the monsters out. So, tell me what is happening in your fabulous lives?

THERESA

Well, for beginners, your father and I are exploring the idea of selling this place.

JANICE

Selling the house … ? But … but … why?

THERESA

We're getting old dear, and well … it's time for us to go home.

JANICE

This is home. You've lived here forever.

THERESA

Not quite forever, dear.

JANICE

Where are you going to go?

THERESA

Back to England.

JANICE

England?!?! But you haven't lived there in over
forty years. That's ... that's ... ridiculous.

THERESA

I assure you it's not. Granted it has been a while
but that is where we were born and you know we
go back for a visit at least once a year. It's also a
chance to get away from these dreadful winters.

JANICE

You live in London, Ontario!! It's practically the
same latitude as Northern California.

THERESA

The snow, dear, the snow. After four decades the
novelty has worn off. But it's more than that. You
three are all grown up now. Marshall has settled
down in Germany. We'll be closer to him. We
don't see him much anymore.

JANICE

But Gregory lives in Vancouver. You'll see him
less.

THERESA

Do you disapprove?

JANICE

It's just a bit of a shock. After all this time ...
England?

THERESA

We've got a place already picked out. Near the
Welsh border.

JANICE

> How long have you and Father been planning this?

THERESA

> About a year or so. We felt the time was right.

JANICE

> It's just the idea of strangers living under this roof, that will take some getting used to.

> *LLOYD enters the room, with a shirt on a hanger.*

LLOYD

> Now tell me? Are we going to see the play tonight or should I even bother ironing this shirt again?

JANICE

> So, you're going to England.

LLOYD

> Oh, you told her. Yes, we're going to England. It will be so civilized to get decent pickled onions on a regular basis.

JANICE

> Do Gregory and Marshall know about this?

THERESA

> You're the first.

JANICE

> I'll miss you.

THERESA

No you won't. You'll be too busy with your own
life. Your law practice, this new family you've
discovered, and that man of yours. At the risk of
sounding a little pushy, it would be so nice to
meet the gentleman before we left the country.
What's his name again?

JANICE

Tonto.

LLOYD

You know, I'll just never get used to that name.
In Spanish it means stupid.

JANICE

Don't change the subject. When is all this going
to happen?

LLOYD

Depends on how quickly we can sell the house.
In a perfect world, maybe within the next six
months. Before that horrid snow begins falling.

THERESA

And as I said, it would be so very nice to meet
your young man before we returned to England.

LLOYD

Uh oh, the vultures have started circling. Run,
child, run.

THERESA

So you two are still seeing each other?

JANICE
Yes.

THERESA
And?

JANICE
Nothing.

LLOYD
That almost sounds believable.

THERESA
I thought you had a shirt to iron.

LLOYD
It appears we have a few things to iron out here first.

JANICE
Really, I'd rather not talk about it right now.

LLOYD
A problem. Just as I suspected. This Tonto gentleman, right?

JANICE
No. It's not really a problem.

LLOYD
Well, it's obviously not good news. What does that leave … ?

THERESA
Dear, we only want to help.

LLOYD

You're pregnant.

Both women look at LLOYD with astonishment.

LLOYD

Am I right?

JANICE

How ... how did you know?

THERESA

He's right?!

LLOYD

It's been my experience that women return home with such a noticeable weight on their shoulders under only four conditions. They are broke—and that can't be the case because you were always financially responsible. The second reason would be that you were being abused in some fashion. And I like to think you're smart enough not to put yourself in such a position. The third option would involve you breaking up with that Tonto fellow. But you just said you hadn't. That would only leave you being pregnant ...

THERESA

Pregnant?! I ... I ... don't know what to say. How? Who? When?

LLOYD

I believe you're leaving out what and where.

THERESA
You seem to be taking this ... this shock relatively easy.

LLOYD
She's a grown woman. Grown women in relationships get pregnant. And some that aren't in relationships too. I read the papers. Though I will admit, being a man of my generation, I had hoped there would be that little tradition known as marriage involved. Call me old-fashioned ...

JANICE
I had anticipated that too. But sometimes you deal with the situation as it develops.

THERESA
Is it this Tonto fellow?

JANICE
Yes.

LLOYD
Does he know?

JANICE
No.

LLOYD
Don't you think you should tell him? I believe notification of the father is still practiced in some parts of this country.

JANICE
I know. It just took me by surprise ... I ... guess you could say I panicked.

THERESA
Why?

JANICE
It would take too long to get into.

LLOYD
I have a question. Should we consider this pregnancy good news, or bad?

JANICE
Do you need an answer now?

LLOYD
I see.

THERESA
Are you sure there's not some health concerns to consider? I mean, dear, you're not exactly in your prime child-bearing years. Especially for a first child.

JANICE
I'm not that old, mother. Thirty-seven is still relatively risk free. But the annoying thing is, I'm already feeling a craving for unusually flavoured ice creams.

THERESA
Oh that's just a fallacy. I never experienced any cravings. Did I, darling?

LLOYD

Don't ask me. I'm trying to blot those pregnancy years out of my memory.

THERESA

You are exaggerating. I wasn't nearly that bad.

LLOYD

Oh the memory is short when the children are tall.

THERESA

What are you going to do? Have you made any plans?

JANICE

I only found out five days ago. I have so much I need to figure out.

LLOYD

Are you going to bring that Tonto fellow into the conversation?

JANICE

At the moment, I think I'll just go grab something to eat. And no, it's not a craving. It's something called lunch. You might want to consider some yourselves.

JANICE exits.

THERESA

Our daughter is with child.

LLOYD

So it seems.

They pause.

LLOYD

I take it this means there'll be no play tonight.

THERESA

Lloyd, she's changed so much in the past two years. I almost don't recognize her. Do you think she'll be okay?

LLOYD

Oh Theresa, you ask so many questions.

THERESA

And you answer so few of them.

JANICE yells to them from the kitchen.

JANICE

Do you have any wild rice?

THERESA

In the kitchen? Uh, no. I don't believe so.

JANICE

That's okay. It would take too long to prepare. Maybe I'll have a tuna sandwich or something. (*pause*) And you have ice cream!

LLOYD

Tuna fish with mango ice cream. She is pregnant.

THERESA

I really wish we could meet this Tonto fellow.

LLOYD

Maybe there's a reason we haven't met him.
Maybe she's ashamed of him.

THERESA

If my memory is correct, your future possibilities
weren't exactly overflowing when I first met you.
On our first date, you were one pound and six
shillings short for dinner I believe.

LLOYD

Why do you remember these inconsequential
little details?

THERESA

If life is worth living, it's worth remembering.

LLOYD

Regardless, this is all Janice's matter and while I
may have a few reservations about the manner in
which this has all happened, I refuse to fit the
stereotype of the meddling parent.

THERESA

But ...

LLOYD

But nothing. Good meddling involves far too
much exertion and I'm getting much too old to
consider it anymore. So if you will excuse me, I
have a shirt to iron on the off chance we do
make it to the play.

THERESA
There is a far cry between a meddling parent,
and a concerned one.

LLOYD
Not in my dictionary.

JANICE enters the room carrying her lunch.

JANICE
I left some of the tuna on the counter if
anybody's hungry.

THERESA
Your father seems to think I'm meddling.

JANICE
Why? What did you do?

THERESA
Nothing.

LLOYD
Yet.

JANICE
There is nothing to meddle in. This is my
decision. My responsibility.

THERESA
I just want to be here for you. That's all.

JANICE
You are. That's why I came home. That's why I'm
here. I just need some time to get my mind
together.

LLOYD
Fine. Our house is your house. Do you want to
come to the play tonight?

JANICE
You know, I'd love to. Maybe that's what I need.
A night out. I can't remember the last time I saw
Caesar and Cleopatra.

LLOYD
Tickets for three it is.

> *LLOYD exits.*

JANICE
It will be fun.

THERESA
Yes it will. And Janice, my daughter, welcome
home.

Scene Five

Although in a different location, ANNE *is again closer physically to* JANICE *who is seated onstage, again listening intently.*

ANNE

You should have seen me while I was carrying you. I was just a bundle of energy. I was cleaning this, and washing that. Do you know how much cleaning and washing you can do in nine months! I wanted to get our little house ready 'cause I knew once you arrived, I'd be pretty busy looking after you. Frank was busy fixing up the storeroom to give you your own room. We didn't have much money back then, so we had to do everything ourselves. So, there I was, sewing madly, making all kinds of baby clothes. All of them white. Back then there was no way of finding out if you were going to be a boy or a girl, not that we'd want to know, mind you. That seemed to be part of the fun, not knowing. If you can call being pregnant fun. My plan was once you were born, I would use the money I had stashed away to buy some dye. And then I would dye all the clothes pink or blue, depending on you. Being poor can teach you to be plenty resourceful. Frank had your room ready for you in about a month, and I had more than enough clothes for you, and your brother Paul and sister Barb when their time came. And all this time, I had but two problems with you. You know, I couldn't get enough pickerel. Your father had a way of frying it with onions that made my mouth water. When he wasn't fixing up that storeroom, I had him out on that lake bringing me home some fish all the time. I must have went through at least two whole pickerel a day. I'm sure of it. I also had heartburn something fierce. I'm sure it had nothing to do with the fish 'cause it had never caused me no pain before. But somehow, from deep inside my stomach, you found a way to reach way up and give me heartburn. And nothing would get rid of it. Your father was happy and whistling, waiting for the day you would join us. Me, I gained a whole new respect for my mother. Twelve children and I wondered how she could have any heart left. I asked her about the heartburn and she said it wasn't a burn, it was a glow. My heart was glowing for you.

Scene Six

It is later that same day. JANICE is asleep on the
couch. At one point, she moans and rolls over.
LLOYD is standing by a doorway watching his
daughter. THERESA enters, notices her husband,
and joins him.

THERESA
What's wrong?

LLOYD
When I retired, that's pretty well what I assumed
I'd be spending much of the day doing.

THERESA
Let her enjoy her nap, God knows she'll have
precious little time once the baby comes.

JANICE rolls over again, moaning.

She seems to be having a dream.

LLOYD
Or two.

THERESA
It didn't seem all that long ago she only took up
half that couch.

LLOYD
Sorry to add a note of reality but it wasn't that
couch. We bought a new one fifteen years ago,
remember?

THERESA

It was the same colour.

LLOYD

I know you said let her sleep but we really should be getting ready to leave. We have dinner reservations and the play is in a few hours.

THERESA

Oh you and your precious Shaw. You wake her, then.

LLOYD

Very well.

LLOYD walks over to the sleeping JANICE.

Janice, it's time to wake up.

JANICE mumbles something.

THERESA

What was that?

LLOYD

I believe she said that she didn't want to go to school today.

THERESA

Haven't heard that one in a while.

LLOYD

Janice, we have to get ready for the theatre. Wake up.

Slowly, JANICE wakes up.

JANICE

What … what's wrong?

LLOYD

Nothing. We have to leave for the theatre soon.
You should start getting ready.

JANICE

Oh, the play. Yeah, sorry, that hot tub really took
it out of me. Okay. I'll get ready.

THERESA

It sounded like you were having a dream?
Anything interesting?

JANICE

Too interesting.

LLOYD

Ladies, the time.

JANICE

Right. Be ready in a second.

JANICE exits the room.

LLOYD

What about you?

THERESA

Way ahead of you.

She models for him.

Sufficient for Shaw?

LLOYD
Very Cleopatra-ish.

THERESA
Should I get an asp to go with it?

LLOYD
No need. I always said you had a nice asp.

THERESA
I must wear this dress more often then.

LLOYD
My goodness, we may actually be ready on time for both dinner and the curtain. The Fates must have the day off.

The doorbell rings.

THERESA
Then again.

LLOYD
You're sure Marshall is in Germany and Gregory is in Vancouver? We don't have any other children, do we?

THERESA
The night's young, darling.

THERESA opens the door to reveal TONTO, JANICE's Native boyfriend.

Good afternoon.

TONTO
Um, how ... do you do?

LLOYD
Who is it?

THERESA
It's a gentleman and he appears to be Native.

LLOYD
Must be one of Janice's friends.

TONTO
I don't suppose Janice might be here? I mean I
saw her car and all ...

THERESA
I'm sorry but you are ...

TONTO
My name is Tonto Hunter. I'm a good friend of
Grace ... Janice's.

THERESA
So you're the famous Tonto!! Well, Mr. Hunter,
I've been led to believe that you're a little more
than just a good friend. She's had good friends
before but ...

TONTO
Pardon?

THERESA
Nothing. Please do come in.

TONTO enters the house.

TONTO
You have a very nice house. Exactly how I
pictured it.

THERESA
Darling, come and meet Tonto Hunter, Janice's
... friend.

LLOYD
Tonto! Thee Tonto? Well, good day, sir. Your
work precedes you.

TONTO
Uh thank you. Is Gra ... Janice here? I've come a
long way looking for her.

LLOYD
She's upstairs getting dressed.

TONTO
Thank God I've found her. Is she okay? I was
getting a little worried.

THERESA
Is everything okay with you two?

TONTO
To tell you the truth, I'm not sure. I woke up
yesterday morning, and she was gone. Nothing
but a lukewarm pillow left behind. She'd been
having trouble sleeping lately but she wouldn't
tell me why. She left her clothes behind,
everything. I left messages at her apartment, her
cell phone is turned off. Nothing. Barb, her
sister, didn't know where she was.

THERESA
How did you know she was here?

TONTO
Process of elimination. This was the only place I could think of that was left.

THERESA
Well, no need to worry. She's quite fine. She'll be down in a moment. Can I get you a drink or something?

TONTO
No thanks but I could use the bathroom. It's been a long drive and too much Tim Hortons coffee.

LLOYD
(*pointing*) Right over there.

TONTO
Thank you.

TONTO exits.

LLOYD
So that's him.

THERESA
So it seems. Good-looking chap.

LLOYD
You think so?

THERESA
I have to. He's the father of our grandchild.

LLOYD
Needs a haircut though.

THERESA
Oh Lloyd, you've been saying that since the sixties. That's the way it is now. Especially Native people. I saw it on a television show. They all have long hair. Don't you be racist!

LLOYD
Commenting on hair isn't racist.

THERESA
I suppose I should get Janice.

LLOYD
This won't take too long, will it? It's almost 5:00.

THERESA
You are such an optimist, darling.

THERESA exits.

LLOYD
Scotch helps.

TONTO exits the bathroom.

TONTO
That's much better. Somehow returning to the Earth what she gave up to you can be kinda satisfying, don't you think?

LLOYD
I've never viewed a trip to the bathroom as being so spiritual.

TONTO

You should. Your bathroom is almost shrine-like.

LLOYD

My wife has a knack for decorating.

TONTO

I can tell. There's a lot of Grace ... I mean Janice's apartment here. Must run in the family.

LLOYD

Why do you call Janice "Grace"?

TONTO

Oh, that was her birth name. The one her birth mother Anne, gave her. Back in Otter Lake we sort of took it upon ourselves to re-christen Janice "Grace." Nothing personal.

LLOYD

Oh yes, I remember her saying something about that some months back. I used to call Janice "Princess" when she was young.

TONTO

As in Princess ... Grace?

LLOYD

There's a certain amount of irony to it I suppose, as well as some old world charm.

TONTO

As opposed to some new world charm?

LLOYD pours himself a drink.

LLOYD
Speaking of names ... Tonto. Is that an old family name?

TONTO
It's a nickname.

LLOYD
How did you get it?

TONTO
It's an ancient Indian secret buried in myth and legend, dealing with many sacred and spiritual rituals that would take a lifetime of study to appreciate.

LLOYD
Are you sure I can't get you a drink?

TONTO
No thank you.

LLOYD
My father always warned me not to trust a man who won't sit down and have a drink with you.

TONTO
Really?! My father always warned me to beware of white men offering you alcohol.

LLOYD
I take it that was a joke.

TONTO
That's just my way of saying I don't drink. I'm
sort of what you might call a recovering
alcoholic. Having a social drink kind of defeats
the purpose of A.A.

LLOYD
Well put. How long have you been a member?

TONTO
Going on five years.

LLOYD
Has it been difficult?

TONTO
Not really. Staying drunk was harder. But that's
just me. Enjoy your scotch.

There is a silence.

And Janice?

LLOYD
Theresa has gone to get her.

TONTO
Thank you. I'm sorry for just barging in on you
like this but ...

LLOYD
I quite understand. As you said, you were
concerned.

TONTO
London's quite a lovely city. I haven't ...

THERESA and JANICE enter the room. JANICE is a little better dressed than before, but hasn't finished her transformation yet.

JANICE

It's a little tight about the tummy but ...

She looks up and sees TONTO standing beside her father. She freezes.

Tonto!

TONTO

Ahneen. Awak-ni-ge? (Hello. How are you?)

JANICE

Um ... Awak-ge. Keen? (Fine. You?)

TONTO

Hmmm ... Awak-ge. (Fine.)

THERESA

I didn't know you picked up another language?

JANICE

I haven't, really. Just some of the more important and common phrases and words.

TONTO

Oh come on. You know more than that. She's a fast learner.

JANICE

What are you doing here?

TONTO

I'd like to know that myself.

JANICE

I was going to call you.

TONTO

Do you want me to go home and wait for the phone to ring?

JANICE

That won't be necessary. I'm glad to see you. I see you've met my parents.

TONTO

Yep. Not exactly how I expected to meet them but ... (*pause*) So, what's new?

JANICE

Tonto, we have to talk.

TONTO

There are no scarier words in the English language, or Ojibway for that matter, then when a woman says to you, "Tonto, we have to talk." Am I in trouble?

JANICE

Don't be silly.

TONTO

Are you in trouble?

LLOYD

Haven't heard it phrased like that in a long time.

THERESA

Lloyd, perhaps we should adjourn elsewhere for the duration of this potentially earth-shattering moment.

LLOYD

Like the theatre?

THERESA

Maybe tomorrow night.

LLOYD

(*dramatically*) And tomorrow. And tomorrow. And tomorrow.

THERESA and LLOYD exit.

TONTO

So what's up? You disappear like the wind. I scour the Earth looking for you. You say I haven't done anything wrong but there's something definitely written on your face. And I don't know why. Should we play twenty questions?

JANICE

It's a little more complicated than that. Actually in some ways it's very simple. Oh Tonto, I don't know what I mean. It's all so confusing. I thought I'd put all this turmoil behind me.

TONTO

What is so confusing? Grace, let me in. I can't do anything to help from out here.

JANICE

I've been having dreams.

TONTO

Uh huh?

JANICE

It's more than that. A lot more. I'm actually
worried about what it might mean. That's part of
what's so scary.

TONTO

No, dreams are good. They are put there to be
helpful, to assist us in our path through life.
Don't be afraid of them, embrace and cherish
them. Some believe they are the voice of the
Creator or maybe a window into your future. Or
past. You shouldn't fear them. (*pause*) Unless
they tell you to climb up a water tower and start
shooting people.

JANICE doesn't respond.

That's not actually what they're telling you, are
they?

JANICE laughs.

Oh Good. See Grace laugh. See Grace smile. See
Grace share with Tonto.

JANICE

These dreams …

TONTO

Yes?

JANICE

These dreams ... are about Anne.

TONTO

I asked this before and I'm going to ask it again. Uh huh?

JANICE

It's what Anne is talking about.

TONTO

Sharing shouldn't be this hard. What about Anne in your dreams?

JANICE

She's telling me stories. Stories about when she was pregnant with me. I can't move or speak. I'm frozen, just sitting there, listening, watching. I want to run away but I can't even turn my head. I can see her so clearly. I can hear her voice. I can even smell her, the aroma of the talcum powder she wore that one time I met her. That's the problem. I don't know why I'm having these dreams! I shouldn't be. I knew the woman for ... for barely an hour. One lousy hour! And maybe two short phone calls afterwards. Then she died, Tonto, she died. In these dreams, she's not dead. She keeps telling me about carrying me, being my mother, and what it meant to her. Why is she doing this? Why am I dreaming her?

TONTO

Take it easy. We can deal with this.

JANICE

What do you mean "we"? "We" aren't having the dreams. "We" don't see her there night after night, smiling that sweet smile.

TONTO

First of all, I'm on your side, remember? There's no need to take a chunk out on me. And second, you're viewing this as a bad thing. Most people whose mother has passed on might view this as a positive thing, a chance to see their mother one last time. Resolve some unfinished business or seek some form of guidance.

JANICE

Will you spare me the New Age analysis, just for once!

TONTO

Wait a minute. This isn't New Age stuff, this is Old Age, Ancient Age. New Age people are playing in a shallow pool, the stuff I've been taught is way in the deep end.

JANICE

Well goody for you but I don't ...

TONTO

Ooh somebody's cranky. By the way, you look very nice in that dress. I've never seen you wear it before. It does look a little tight though.

JANICE

That's another thing.

TONTO
    There's more?

JANICE
    Oh I haven't even scratched the surface.

TONTO
    Well, scratch away.

JANICE
    There's been … a development.

TONTO
    And I thought treaty negotiations took forever.
    What kind of development?

JANICE
    Where to begin …

TONTO
    Does it have anything to do with the dreams?

JANICE
    I'm almost positive.

TONTO
    That's a beginning. Well, whatever it is, let me
    help.

JANICE
    Tonto …

        *JANICE leans against the couch looking for
        support.*

JANICE

    I don't feel so good.

TONTO

    You don't look so good either. Is that why you're
    here? Are you sick with something?

JANICE

    Tonto, there are things happening in this
    universe that neither of us expected.

TONTO

    It's called life. I read about it somewhere.

JANICE

    Well, it's happening here. Now.

TONTO

    For the third and last time. Uh huh?

JANICE

    Here goes ...

> *Suddenly JANICE collapses on the couch. She is in*
> *great pain, centred around her mid-section.*

JANICE

    Oh Jesus! Oh God!

TONTO

    Grace! What ... You okay?

JANICE

    No! Get my parents! My parents.

TONTO
Okay, okay. Just stay here!

JANICE
Where the hell am I gonna go?!

TONTO runs to the doorway and yells.

TONTO
Yo, Mr. Wirth. Mrs. Wirth, something's wrong
with Grace ... Janice ... your daughter.

He returns to JANICE's side.

TONTO
Where does it hurt?

JANICE
Down here. All over. Oh God, do something.

TONTO
Want me to rub your temples?

JANICE
I don't have a headache.

LLOYD and THERESA rush in.

LLOYD
What's the matter?

TONTO
She collapsed. I don't know ...

THERESA
Honey, are you okay?

JANICE
    It hurts, Mother, it hurts.

THERESA
    Lloyd?

LLOYD
    I'll call 911.

TONTO
    Is there something I can do?

THERESA
    Toss me that pillow.

>   *TONTO complies while THERESA attempts to make
>   her daughter more comfortable.*

JANICE
    It can't be my appendix. I had that out.

THERESA
    Janice dear, it may be something more serious
    than that.

JANICE
    The baby?

THERESA
    Possibly.

TONTO
    What baby?

LLOYD
> The ambulance is on its way. Just a few minutes they said.

THERESA
> Did you hear that, dear? They're on their way.

TONTO
> What baby?

THERESA
> Lloyd, get my jacket and put it by the door. Also my address book on the desk. We'll need our doctor's phone number and ...

TONTO
> WHAT BABY!

LLOYD
> What is he babbling about?

THERESA
> I don't think Janice got around to telling him.

LLOYD
> Oh for the love of ... Janice is pregnant. With your child. End of story. Now make yourself useful and go watch the driveway for the ambulance.

TONTO
> She's gonna have a baby?

LLOYD
> The man catches on fast, doesn't he?

JANICE
Tonto ... Tonto ...

TONTO
Huh? What?

JANICE
I meant to tell you differently. Really I did.

TONTO
Um ... Just take care of yourself. That's what's important right now.

THERESA
Where is that damn ambulance?

LLOYD
Tonto, please, go watch the driveway and guide them in. Now!

Confused and stunned, TONTO manages to make his way to the door.

JANICE
Tonto! How does this make you feel?

THERESA
Janice, this really isn't the time ...

JANICE
It's important. Tonto ... ?

TONTO
I think I have a stomach ache.

JANICE screams in pain. TONTO screams sympathetically. The lights go down.

End of Act One.

ACT TWO

Scene One

*Lights up on the Wirth house. It is quiet and in a
partial state of disarray. Silence. Then noise
coming from the front door. It opens and
THERESA, LLOYD and TONTO enter. They all
make room as JANICE enters. They surround her
in attempts to be helpful.*

THERESA
Watch your step, dear?

LLOYD
Just a little further to the couch, Princess.

TONTO
Do you want to lean on me? You can if you want
to.

JANICE
For God's sakes people, give me some room.

TONTO/THERESA/LLOYD
Everybody step back. Give her some room. She
needs some air.

> *JANICE sits down on the couch and the three stand
> around her, concerned, watching.*

JANICE
Is there a problem?

TONTO/THERESA/LLOYD
No, no problem. Do you need anything? I could
warm up some soup?

JANICE
(*loudly*) I'm all right. It was just a false alarm.

THERESA
Still, the doctor did say ...

JANICE
That I'll be okay. Just no more hot tubs.

THERESA
You were lucky, young lady. Hot tubs and
pregnant women do not mix. You could have lost
the child.

JANICE
But I didn't. And will you all quit looking at me?
It makes me nervous.

THERESA
Well, then, who's up for some tea?

LLOYD
Smashing.

TONTO
I'd love some.

THERESA
Janice?

JANICE
That would be nice.

THERESA exits the room.

TONTO
Are you sure you're okay?

JANICE
For the fourteenth time, yes.

TONTO
Just asking. Who would have thought hot tubs could be dangerous? I mean especially since the baby will be water clan.

LLOYD
What are you talking about?

TONTO
You see, in Ojibway culture, the child usually takes the father's clan. Mine. Otter to be specific.

JANICE
I didn't know that. What am I?

TONTO

I believe you're an … Aries.

LLOYD

I see the world of political correctness hasn't
made its way into this clan issue.

TONTO

Actually I never thought it was completely fair to
simply ignore the mother's clan. Or the reverse
in the Iroquois tradition where it's the mother's
clan that is passed down and the father's clan
that's not mentioned. I always felt the clan system
should be more like what they do at universities.
You should have a major and a minor. That way
you honour both sides. Take me, for instance,
I'm majoring in Otter but minoring in Turtle.

LLOYD

Where do you find these men?

THERESA enters the room.

THERESA

I forgot to ask Tonto what he would like in his
tea?

TONTO

Some honey would be nice.

THERESA

Mr. Wirth, I shall need you for the honey jar.

LLOYD

Luggage and jars. That's all I'm good for in this house.

LLOYD and THERESA exit.

JANICE

Seriously, Tonto. Do I have a clan?

TONTO

Every family has a clan.

JANICE

Like the Scots?

TONTO

Aye, lassie but that's not important now. Why didn't you tell me you were pregnant? Don't tell me it slipped your mind.

JANICE

I didn't know what to tell you, or how. Sometimes with men you never know how they will react. I've seen men react to the news they were going to be fathers like it was just another mouth to feed. Others react like it was the second coming of ... Christ!

JANICE realizes she is repeating ANNE's words. She stops quickly.

TONTO

What? I was listening.

JANICE

I was just saying that this is not something I was expecting at this stage of my life.

TONTO

I would have been there for you. I still am there for you. Or here. Or wherever you want me to be.

JANICE

Tonto, so much has changed in such a short period of time. Not long ago I lived in my own little world, working, doing my thing. And then suddenly, everything changed. I discovered a whole new family, a new community that wanted me to call it home, a different way of looking at things. But Anne died before I could straighten things out.

TONTO

But look where you are now. It took a bit of doing, but you're pretty much on the right path now. You, my lovely, are in the unique position of straddling both worlds. One foot in this house, one in Otter Lake.

JANICE

That's four hundred kilometres away.

TONTO

Yeah, admittedly that's a pretty wide stride. Just don't expect to do it all at once. If you try to, you could hurt yourself. It's like a meal, take things in servings, one at a time; appetizers, salads, vegetables, meat, desserts, all spread out over the evening. It makes things a lot easier.

JANICE

You've got a metaphor for everything, don't you?

TONTO

So, you've got a baby in you. How does that make you feel?

JANICE

Nervous. Scared. Worried. How do you feel?

TONTO

Delighted, pleased, happy. Once the initial shock wore off.

JANICE

Obviously we're looking at this from two different perspectives.

TONTO

Maybe but forgive me if I ask the obvious. Actually there are two obvious questions burning inside my head. First of all, are you going to keep the baby? And second, regardless of the first decision, how does this affect us?

JANICE

You want the child, don't you?

TONTO

Oh yes.

There is a pause as JANICE makes a decision.

JANICE
So do I.

TONTO
YES!

JANICE
As for you …

TONTO
Yes … ?

JANICE
I think I'll keep you around. You're cheaper than therapy.

TONTO
It has often been said that mothers are truly wise.

THERESA enters carrying some tea.

THERESA
Here we go. Are Native people fond of tea?

TONTO
I've heard of some.

THERESA pours a cup for TONTO and JANICE.

JANICE
Thank you.

TONTO
Meegwetch.

JANICE nudges him.

TONTO

Thank you very much, Mrs. Wirth. So how does it feel, knowing you're going to be a grandmother?

THERESA

Quite liberating actually. I never know what to buy you or your brothers for Christmas anymore. Now at least I can buy you baby goods for the next several years.

JANICE

You're so practical.

THERESA

You'll find that with motherhood. The very minute before you give birth will be the last time you consider this Earth a safe place. After that, you will view everything around you as potential danger for your child. Enjoy these last few months, my dear, they'll be your last carefree days.

JANICE

You're not exactly painting a rosy picture, Mother. I'd like to look forward to this, if you don't mind.

THERESA

As well you should but it's a great responsibility. And with responsibility comes awareness and duty. That's all I'm saying.

TONTO

I agree with your mother. Too many people take having kids too lightly.

THERESA
Indeed.

TONTO
That's why I think you should consider moving back to the Reserve permanently.

THERESA
I beg your pardon?

JANICE
Not this again. We've been over this before. I'm a lawyer. Where the hell am I going to find work in Otter Lake?

TONTO
There's the land claim. That claim will keep many a lawyer well fed and cosy for the next millennium.

JANICE
I'm an entertainment lawyer. There's a world of difference. I don't know the first thing about land claims.

TONTO
I hope you're not thinking of raising our child in Toronto?! That place eats people. I think it was built on an immigrant burial ground or something.

THERESA
I have a simply wonderful idea. Brilliant in fact. Why not buy this old place?

TONTO
> Here?

THERESA
> I think it's safe to say I have some influence with
> the previous owner. I'm sure we could easily
> manage something. You yourself said you would
> hate this house to go to strangers. Think of it,
> another generation of Wirths to occupy these
> halls.

TONTO
> Thanks but …

JANICE
> Here? I never thought of that. You realize I
> couldn't possibly come up with its true market
> value immediately. I'm just a struggling lawyer
> who drives a four-year-old Saab.

THERESA
> You should talk to your father. You know he
> could never say no to you.

JANICE
> Except about my curfew.

THERESA
> He did lift it last year, darling.

> *Excited, JANICE exits in search of her father.*

> I believe in happy endings, don't you?

TONTO
I'll let you know when I find one. I'm in a bit of a pickle here.

THERESA
Oh, how so?

TONTO
I was actually hoping Janice would consider bringing up the baby in Otter Lake.

THERESA
Good heavens, why would you want to raise the baby there?

TONTO
Because it's my home. Janice's home too.

THERESA
You're standing in Janice's home. Don't you think this city would be a better place for the child? It has better medical facilities, education ...

TONTO
There are different kinds of medicine and education.

THERESA
If you want this child to succeed in this world ...

TONTO
Which world?

THERESA
What does that mean?

TONTO

> I mean no disrespect but I would just like the
> baby to have some of the benefits that Janice
> didn't. That's all.

THERESA

> Benefits?! She had a full stomach, clothes on her
> back, and two loving parents. What more could a
> child need?

TONTO

> Maybe a culture and people. A place where he or
> she fits in.

THERESA

> Janice fit in. We went out of our way to show no
> favouritism. We saw her no differently from
> Gregory and Marshall.

TONTO

> But she is. She's a member of the great Ojibway
> nation.

THERESA

> We acknowledged that. We were quite open with
> her about her aboriginal heritage.

TONTO

> What exactly does "open" mean?

THERESA

> Letting her know she was adopted.

TONTO

I don't think that was much of a stretch of
deduction. Not a particularly strong family
resemblance.

THERESA

We actually didn't know she was Ojibway. Back in
those days, the authorities didn't bother to
inform us of those details.

TONTO

Did you say details?! The fact that Grace ended
up in this house was part of an assimilation
program instituted by the federal government.
Part of a larger plan to destroy the Native races
and integrate us into the larger melting pot of
Canada. Pass the honey please.

THERESA

I think you're exaggerating.

TONTO

It wasn't your children they took.

THERESA

Am I to understand that you are accusing Lloyd
and myself of ... of ... some form of cultural
genocide?

TONTO

Not over tea. Do you know that in Manitoba,
Native people are twelve percent of the overall
population, but they make up seventy percent of
the children in social service? Look, Grace has
told me all about you two. Good stuff. You were

good parents to her. A lot better than most, believe me.

THERESA

Thank you.

TONTO

And as her partner, I would like to thank you for the great job you've done. But there are huge holes in her education, as an aboriginal person. Gaps that are all to frequent in adoptees like Grace. I know.

THERESA

Well, Janice, as she's known in this house, turned out pretty fine if you ask me. A beautiful, fine, independent woman. A skilled lawyer in a top notch legal firm. Not much to be ashamed of there. Or do Native people look down on success?

TONTO

No, not success. She's done pretty good for herself. I don't deny that but where I come from, the community is more important than the individual.

THERESA

I know what's going on in these communities of yours. I watch the news. I know the incredibly high rates of suicide, the living conditions, the economic reality. The high infant mortality rate. It's tragic but it is certainly not the environment I want my grandchild raised in.

TONTO

Don't you dare throw statistics at me. They've done more damage than most diseases. Yes, some of those things are true. But you're only commenting on the negative stuff. And our communities are taking steps to fight these tragedies. But look beyond the headlines. Why these things have happened. It's because the government, its agents and its policies put us in positions to fail.

LLOYD enters, smiling.

LLOYD

Theresa, start packing. I do believe we have a buyer.

THERESA

Darling, do you consider us to be fit parents?

LLOYD

Excuse me?

THERESA

It seems our young friend here is under the assumption that we were negligent in raising our daughter.

LLOYD

All this after only four hours in our house.

TONTO

I'm being misquoted here. I didn't say anything like that. What I was saying was simply Grace ... or Janice, wherever she may be geographically at any given point, needs to learn a little bit more than what was available to her here, growing up. And I would like that for our child too. See, nothing bad.

LLOYD
And what exactly do you believe we have denied our daughter?

TONTO
A knowledge of who she is and where she comes from. Aboriginally speaking, of course. There's some tea.

THERESA
Darling, do you think Janice knows who she is?

LLOYD
She'd better. We can't afford to send her back through law school again. Does this have anything to do with that clan stuff you were mentioning earlier?

TONTO
Partially.

LLOYD
If it will please the both of you, then give her a clan.

TONTO
That's not how it's done. But that's exactly what I'm talking about. Janice doesn't know her clan, barely speaks coherent Ojibway ...

LLOYD
	Question: Is it mandatory to speak fluent Ojibway
	to be officially recognized as Native? Do all
	Ojibways speak Ojibway? Is there a secret
	password or something?

TONTO
	No but ...

LLOYD
	I didn't think so. So while you're penalizing us,
	and Janice by association, for her not knowing
	Ojibway, it's okay with you that there are a
	multitude of Ojibways out there in Ojibway
	homes that don't speak the language. Would you
	be as harsh on their parents as with us?

TONTO
	You're a lawyer, aren't you?

LLOYD
	I take it you don't like lawyers?

TONTO
	Guns don't kill people, lawyers do.

LLOYD
	I see.

		There is an awkward silence.

THERESA
	Lloyd?

LLOYD

It's alright, Theresa. Everyone's entitled to their opinion.

TONTO

Look, Janice was raised to be a very good white woman. Now she needs to learn to be a very good Ojibway woman. And I want that for our child. How's that?

THERESA

Are the two mutually exclusive of each other?

TONTO

I'd answer that if I knew what it meant.

THERESA

Listen, young man, I think you'll find few women as competent and as strong as our Janice.

TONTO

Yes but ...

THERESA

This cultural superiority you champion makes no difference to the person underneath. It's just fancy clothing that has no relation to the individual.

TONTO

I think ...

THERESA

And for you to assume that Janice and her child will not be as well off as say ... your brethren

raised in your environment is incredibly
presumptuous and I resent it.

TONTO
    No let me …

THERESA
    Have you ever raised a child, stayed up 'til three
    in the morning when they've had chicken pox?
    Tried to comfort them when they've had a
    broken arm and don't understand why they have
    to wear a cast?

TONTO
    No, I haven't …

THERESA
    Well I have. When you've put in the hours, done
    the work, stayed up a hundred nights in the
    name of parenthood, then you will be in the
    position to criticize us about how to raise a child.
    Otherwise, you are driving a car without a
    license.

TONTO
    Now can …

THERESA
    Janice is my daughter and you have no right to
    tell me I didn't raise her properly. I loved her
    and that was not evil. Mr. Hunter, you may go
    now.

TONTO
    Pardon?

THERESA

I have said all I have to say. The argument is over.
You may leave our house.

TONTO

But what about ... ?

THERESA

She has two loving parents to look after her, ones
that do not find her wanting.

TONTO

I can't just go. Mr. Wirth?

LLOYD

Son, I may be the lawyer in this family, but she's
the judge. Best be on your way.

THERESA walks over and opens the door.

THERESA

Anytime you are ready, Mr. Hunter.

TONTO

But Janice ...

THERESA

Thank you for coming. We'll give your regrets to
Janice. Have a nice day.

TONTO

Just one more ...

THERESA

I don't think so.

THERESA closes the door in his face.

LLOYD
> Theresa, are you … ?

THERESA
> There are two things in this house I do not
> tolerate. One—rudeness. Second—foam pillows.

> *THERESA exits.*

LLOYD
> Now that's how Britain conquered itself an
> empire.

> *JANICE enters the room carrying her glass of tea
> and another sandwich.*

JANICE
> I guess there's no point in me staying on the diet.
> There might be an upside to this after all. What
> do you say to pizza for dinner tonight, triple
> cheese, onions and pepperoni? Garlic bread.
> Caesar salad …

LLOYD
> Please don't mention Caesar.

JANICE
> Where's Tonto?

> *THERESA, not finding JANICE in the other room,
> re-enters.*

THERESA
> Good. Janice dear …

JANICE

    He's not in the bathroom.

THERESA

    If you're looking for Mr. Hunter, he left the
    house.

JANICE

    Did he say where he was going?

THERESA

    He didn't. In fact, he was very rude.

JANICE

    Tonto?! Tonto is never rude.

THERESA

    Obviously you don't know the father of your
    child as well as you thought. He actually accused
    us of improperly raising you.

JANICE

    Tonto?!

LLOYD

    I'm afraid it's true. He thinks that we've made
    you into a white person which to him appears to
    be a great tragedy. At least that's the gist of his
    argument as we understood it. We felt his
    criticisms were severely impolite.

JANICE

    Did he say if he was coming back?

THERESA

He really didn't say much as he was leaving. Dear, we're sorry it came to this.

JANICE

I've got to find him.

THERESA

Really, dear, it's not that necessary ...

JANICE

You don't understand. There's more to this than you can comprehend. All my life I've been wondering who I was, where I belonged and why I was here.

LLOYD

Everybody wonders those things at some point in their life.

JANICE

Not like me. I grew up in this wonderful home with a wonderful family. But there was always something missing. Something I was searching for even though I didn't know it.

THERESA

Surely you don't think that man ...

JANICE

It's more than Tonto, more than just any one person, it's ... it's ... you both have lived in Canada for over forty years, yet you are planning to move back to England to retire. Why?

LLOYD
> It's our home.

JANICE
> Exactly. I can't argue with that because in my
> own way I can understand it. When you're back
> in England, you'll feel completed. I want that
> feeling before I retire.

LLOYD
> And what does this have to do with Tonto?

JANICE
> I'm his kemosaabe.

> *JANICE exits.*

THERESA
> Darling, we shouldn't let her go. She just got
> back from the hospital.

. LLOYD
> Maybe it's time we let her go. She's not a princess
> anymore.

Scene Two

ANNE, much closer to JANICE, is talking.

ANNE

You were born on a Thursday. There was lots of
snow on the ground but the smell of spring was
definitely in the air. It was a day that made you
feel good. Then the contractions came. And
came. And came. You were my first baby and at
first I didn't know exactly what was going on. I
thought maybe it was some bad food or
something. By about the fourth or fifth cramp, it
suddenly dawned on me—pregnant woman with
stomach pains. I get it now. I was twenty years old
at the time—not a particularly knowledgeable
time in any woman's life. I called out to Frank
who was out back chopping wood. I didn't think
he could hear me through the closed windows
and doors but by golly, a father has ways of
hearing his pregnant wife call for him. The
hospital was a good hour away and you were a
fast little baby. Too fast, he figured. Frank picked
me up in his arms and took me to our bedroom.
In that same room where you were conceived,
you were also born. Your thick black hair
announcing your arrival, those lungs of yours
letting me know my life would be forever
changed. At first, Frank was afraid to hold you,
even touch you. His hands were so big, you were
only the size of one of his upper arms. He
thought he'd crush you if he held you the wrong

way. I finally managed to convince him to hold you. I'd never seen him so worried or anxious. But the minute you nestled into his arms, almost disappeared into them, you stopped crying. And that's when he started. Even when I told him they took you away, he never cried. That was the only time I'd ever seen him shed tears. And it took a 7 lb. 4 oz. girl to do it.

Scene Three

LLOYD is sitting in his armchair reading a newspaper.

LLOYD

Theresa, there's a review of *Caesar and Cleopatra* in the paper. It says it's the show of the season. It says "do not miss this production."

THERESA enters the room.

THERESA

In case you haven't noticed, darling, we have our own little drama happening here. Must you obsess over that May-December political love story?

LLOYD

It's a classic.

THERESA

So is a Model T but you don't see me driving one. Where is that woman? It's getting late and the rain has picked up.

LLOYD

And I was the one accused of being over-protective?

THERESA

Read your paper.

LLOYD

I'm every bit as worried as you. I always read the
paper when I feel ineffectual. You know that. It
occupies my mind.

*There is noise at the door and JANICE enters the
room, looking exhausted.*

THERESA

There you are. It's about time, young lady.

JANICE

No, Mother.

THERESA

But dear …

JANICE

I'm cold. I'm wet. And I'm short a man. Those
three things do not put me in a good mood.

THERESA

Your father and I were only trying to help.

JANICE

Yes, I'm familiar with your help.

THERESA

And what does that mean?

JANICE

Remember on my very first date, you told my first
boyfriend not to take me horseback riding that
day because, as you so quaintly put it, I was
having my monthly visitor. We were fifteen years

old. He didn't need to know those details,
Mother.

THERESA

Well I'm sorry if my caring about you is
upsetting.

JANICE

It's not upsetting Mother, but somewhere down
the line you'll have to recognize that I'm
perfectly capable of caring for myself. And
making my own mistakes.

THERESA

But you came home to us. It appeared to us that
you needed some mothering.

JANICE

Mother me tomorrow. Right now, I've got a
missing Ojibway on my mind.

LLOYD

Have you tried any of the local Native
establishments?

JANICE

I never realized how easy it was to hide an
Ojibway in this town. I checked all the places he
would normally hang out at; the Wendy's, Tim
Hortons, the movies, even the bingo hall.
Nothing.

LLOYD

He plays bingo?

JANICE

His whole family does when they're under stress.

LLOYD

Now now, he seems like an able young man. I wouldn't be too worried about him.

JANICE

I know he can look after himself. I'm afraid he went back to Otter Lake.

THERESA

Why don't you phone and inquire?

LLOYD

This isn't like you to be so dependent on a man, father of your child or not.

JANICE

I'm not dependent. Tonto's very important to me, for many reasons. And using the vernacular of the community, he's my man! I wish you hadn't thrown him out.

THERESA

Sweetie, you're shivering. Lloyd, bring me the blanket on the couch.

> *LLOYD does as he's told. They wrap it around the cold JANICE.*

LLOYD

Should we call the doctor again?

JANICE

No, just let me warm up and rest. You know, after checking the bingo hall, I was so cold and tired I fell asleep in the car

THERESA

We should get you to bed.

JANICE

Later. Is there any hot tea left?

THERESA

I believe there are a few drops left at the bottom of the pot.

THERESA pours JANICE a cup.

THERESA

We'll discuss it tomorrow, dear.

JANICE

I might not be here tomorrow.

THERESA

Dear, do you believe we raised you properly?

JANICE is silent for a moment. The silence and the tension mounts.

JANICE

(*hesitantly*) Well … yesss …

THERESA

I see.

JANICE

No you don't. Remember when I was fourteen and we were in the Eastern Townships, just outside of Montreal? We were on vacation, just seeing the sights. We stopped in that small town for a spot of lunch, and went into that café, the one with the curtains you liked. Do you remember what the waitress said to me ...

THERESA

Oh really, Janice, that was so long ago.

JANICE

She said "Quelle bonne petite Sauvage." What a pretty little Indian girl.

THERESA

Times were different then.

JANICE

When Marshall moved to Germany, and we went to visit him in Osnabruck, do you remember how the people acted when they found out I was Native? They kept asking me question after question about aboriginal issues in Canada and I knew nothing. They related to me because of what I was, not who I was. I've reached a stage in my life where what I am and who I am are pretty close to the same thing. It's time for Janice Wirth to know who Grace Wabung is a little bit more. My relationship with you as my parents is not affected. I respect and love you as much as any daughter but this is a different part of my life. Does any of this make sense?

There is silence again.

LLOYD
 I'm one quarter Welsh. Does that count for
 anything?

 JANICE smiles and the tension is partially released.

JANICE
 Mother?

THERESA
 I always thought of myself as your mother.

JANICE
 Yes you will always be my mother.

THERESA
 Will you always be my daughter?

JANICE
 Yes I will.

LLOYD
 Oh for the love of ... Let's not get too maudlin
 here. Some of us haven't had our scotch yet.

THERESA
 Dear, you're not looking well. Perhaps you
 should lie down.

JANICE
 But what about Tonto?

THERESA

No amount of waiting around will speed things up. The famous watched kettle and all.

JANICE

You are such a mother.

JANICE exits the room.

LLOYD

She's a smart girl.

THERESA

I think we can take credit for that, DNA or no DNA.

There is a pause, a beat.

THERESA

I was thinking, while she was gone ... I don't actually know a lot about Native people. Other than the obvious.

LLOYD

I know. There weren't a lot of them in corporate law either. I think I may have met one at the golf club once but I'm not sure. It didn't come up in conversation. What should we do?

THERESA

I don't know.

Scene Four

ANNE, just a few feet from JANICE.

ANNE

Times were hard back then. Not a lot of opportunity for a decent wage. Especially for an Indian with a new family. We were barely scraping by. Most of our food came from what Frank could catch or hunt himself, and some odd jobs. All good, decent work for a hard-working man. But we didn't have enough money coming in to fix up the house, or buy us the things you needed. So finally, in a moment of desperation, Frank made the only decision he could think of to look after his family. He joined the army. But there were rumours that Indians lost their status when they got discharged. He wouldn't be allowed back on the Reserve. He wouldn't be "Indian" anymore. So Frank never told them he was Indian when he joined. It was the toughest decision that he ever had to make. On the day he had to leave, I packed him a good lunch, almost the last of our good food, so that he wouldn't have to travel all the way on that bus on an empty stomach. I tucked it deep into his duffle bag. I still remember his big, strong arms around me as he hugged me good-bye. Then he looked me in the eyes and made me promise on the Bible, not to tell anybody where he was going, no matter what. Then, he picked you up, very gently. You were still so small in his hands.

And he looked into your smiling face for a long time. I think he was trying to memorize it. Then, he quietly handed you back to me and without saying another word, opened the door and walked to our truck where his brother was waiting to drive him to the bus station. We watched him go until all the dust had settled. We were alone. And on the table, by the door, was the bag of lunch I'd packed for him. He left it behind. For us.

Scene Five

Back in the Wirth home, JANICE is on the phone, talking anxiously.

JANICE
No, huh? (*pause*) I have no idea. I've looked everywhere I could think of. I just thought he might ... (*pause*) Yeah, I'll let you know. Talk to you later, Barb.

JANICE hangs up the phone and absent-mindedly looks out at the pouring rain.

Looks like the thunderbirds are sure out tonight.

There's a flash of lightning. The Wirths enter from outside.

THERESA
Oh hello dear, you're up? We'd thought you'd be asleep.

LLOYD
We picked you up a snack, if you're interested.

JANICE
Not right now. (*beat*) What is it?

LLOYD
A Greek salad and a sandwich. Tuna I believe was your favourite of the day.

JANICE
You two are too good to me.

THERESA

Any sign of Tonto?

JANICE

No. Not yet. I did make some phone calls once I woke up but no luck.

THERESA

While we were out, we picked you up something.

They hand her a large picture-type book.

JANICE

A Pictorial History of the Indians of Canada. Wow, the entire history of aboriginal Canada in two hundred and thirty-seven pages. They must have left out Oka. Why did you get me this?

LLOYD

Janice, when was the Battle of Hastings?

JANICE

1066. Why?

LLOYD

Who won it?

JANICE

William the Conqueror.

THERESA

Who signed the Magna Carta?

JANICE

King John. Is there a specific point to this test?

LLOYD
  Your mother and I were talking over lunch and,
  well, we came to the conclusion that perhaps
  Tonto wasn't entirely incorrect in his assessment.

THERESA
  So we stopped off and bought you a book.

LLOYD
  And the snack.

THERESA
  It was hard to pick one out. Do you know how
  many books are out there written about Native
  people? Dozens! Even hundreds. I was amazed.

LLOYD
  I always told you, Theresa, Anne Perry can only
  go so far.

THERESA
  And Jeffrey Archer is so much more in touch
  with Native people. And did you know this Grey
  Owl fellow was actually British! Archie Belaney!
  You can't get a more cockney name than that!

JANICE
  He actually wasn't cockney. He was very middle-
  class from Hastings.

THERESA
  Oh, well it just goes to show how much there is
  to learn in this world.

JANICE

Thank you for the book. It's very ... big. I don't
know what to say?

LLOYD

Let us know how it ends.

JANICE

I believe the white people win.

JANICE flips through the book.

Oh look, the Ojibway. My people.

The Wirths crowd around the book, looking.

THERESA

Dear, you never looked good in earth tones.

*Somewhere nearby, just outside the house,
TONTO's voice can be heard. He is singing.*

LLOYD

What on Earth ...

JANICE

Tonto ... ?

THERESA

Is that man ... singing ... in the rain?

JANICE

I think it's a '49er.

THERESA

A what?

JANICE

It's a type of song they sing at pow wows. It can also be considered a courting song.

JANICE quickly opens the door, revealing a nervous, soaked TONTO, with a small knapsack, still singing.

TONTO

"When you are far away,
I think of you.
You're beautiful to me.
Hey yah. Hey Yah."

JANICE

You're soaking. Where have you been?

TONTO

Mardi Gras.

JANICE

Get in here. Are you insane?

JANICE physically pulls him in the house.

TONTO

Do you remember when I first sang you that song?

JANICE

Two years ago. At my first pow wow.

TONTO

Your first pow wow, your first Indian taco. Your first round dance ... Our first kiss ...

JANICE

And from one of your ex-girlfriends, my first offer to fight. What has that got to do with anything?

TONTO

I was wandering the city, thinking thoughts and asking myself questions about this very special woman. She has so much wonderful stuff to learn about her people ...

THERESA

Perhaps Lloyd and I ...

TONTO

Thank you but I have some stuff that needs to be said to everyone. First of all, being of aboriginal ancestry does not necessarily prevent you from being a complete idiot.

JANICE

You admit that?

TONTO

Hey, I may be extremely proud of what the Elders have to teach us but they're the first to tell us how human we can be. I realized this as I noticed I had no place to go, no place to be. I knew exactly where I was, but I was lost. The point was driven home by a sudden burst of rain. I believe everything I said but maybe I was interpreting it wrong. It shouldn't cause so much grief. So where does somebody go when they're lost? The movies.

JANICE

You went to the movies? I was sick with worry and you went to the movies!

TONTO

Not quite, I'd seen everything that was playing. I'd seen them all with you. Again, no help. Then I found myself in front of this theatre, the kind that has plays. They were having a matinee and I thought what the hell …

LLOYD

Oh dear God you're kidding …

TONTO

Yeah, it was kind of cool. I'd heard of the central characters, Caesar and Cleopatra …

LLOYD

I give up.

TONTO

A classic story of colonization. I was sitting there, watching the show and things began to dawn on me. Watching these people deal with their problems sort of gave me a better window into my own. Our own. I guess that's why soap operas are so popular.

LLOYD

Caesar and Cleopatra is not a soap opera.

TONTO

Okay, okay, it's not. But what I got out of this cool story of people from different cultures getting together, is that I had forgotten my own teachings. I have been taught that in the end there will not be just Native and non-Native, we will all be one people, one race. And here I was, subdividing the people in this house. I was wrong for doing that. I guess the thing that got me most was that Caesar and Cleopatra had a baby. At that point the gods were shouting in my ear. Granted they were forty years apart in age but the symbolism still works I think. In my eagerness to share what we, the Ojibway, have, I sometimes, unfortunately step on other cultural toes, which is wrong. You took this beautiful little girl, and gave her a good home and a place to grow. I cannot find fault with that. Nor should I. My problem is I've seen a lot of Native children raised in homes that pale by comparison to yours. When you spend a lifetime hearing and healing horror stories, you tend to believe all stories have an undercoating of pain, regardless of how nice the environment may seem. I had no right to inflict my prejudices on you. Especially as a guest in your house. My mother would've whacked me upside my head if she were here. So, I brought a peace offering.

TONTO pulls out a paper bag from his coat pocket and hands it to LLOYD. LLOYD opens it up and pulls out an old-fashioned pseudo-English smoking pipe.

LLOYD
A pipe!

TONTO

Janice told me you like to smoke a pipe
occasionally. I have a different type of pipe. See,
we're not all that different. Tea, pipes ... Janice.

LLOYD

This boy has potential.

JANICE

After all this time, you can still amaze me.

TONTO

I'm not done yet. It's the custom amongst my
people that when a young man is interested in a
young woman, it's his responsibility to curry
favour with her parents.

THERESA

You have a unique way of achieving this, young
man.

TONTO

It's a little rusty. But again, as was the practice
amongst my people, it was my obligation to prove
myself a good provider for your daughter, often
by demonstrating my hunting skills.

JANICE

What have you done?

TONTO

I hereby offer to you, the mother of Janice Wirth,
my Grace Wabung, proof that I can provide for
her. And as the great French lovers would say,
Voilà! There's not really an Ojibway translation.

He reaches into the knapsack and brings out
various materials which he presents to THERESA.

THERESA

What are these? Oh my goodness, blood pudding
... steak and kidney pie ... fish and chips ...

TONTO

From what I understand, all the classics of
English cuisine.

THERESA

And a pint of Guinness.

LLOYD

Hello!

THERESA

You're right, he does have promise.

LLOYD

Not that I'm complaining, mind you, but
Guinness is actually more Irish.

TONTO

Well, you guys all look alike anyways.

JANICE

You did all this for me?

TONTO

When you're wandering the streets of London,
Ontario for several hours thinking about the
woman you love, your opportunities for
distractions are limited. So I found my inner
woman and went shopping.

JANICE

That's the first time I've heard you say the word love.

TONTO

It's been a long day. And if you're a good girl, you might just hear it again.

JANICE

What does a good girl have to do?

TONTO

Everything a bad girl would do but twice as good.

THERESA

Excuse me, we're still here. These are still hot. Wherever did you find them?

TONTO

I'm an Indian, I know how to track things.

LLOYD

A noble endeavour, my boy. But I'm afraid you have us at a disadvantage.

TONTO

That's not necessary ...

THERESA

But it is. We English are capable of our own epiphanies too.

LLOYD

While we still maintain we did all we could to give Janice a proper upbringing ...

THERESA

... perhaps we could have been a little more culturally sensitive. We did however have all the James Fenimore Cooper novels.

TONTO

(*to JANICE*) Is that good?

JANICE

It's a beginning.

THERESA

And if my husband will indulge me, perhaps there is something we can pass on to you.

THERESA exits.

LLOYD

I find it's usually much safer to indulge my wife's whims than not.

TONTO

My father used to say the same thing, except he said it like, "The quietest rabbit lives the longest."

LLOYD

Deep.

THERESA returns carrying a large photo album.

THERESA

These are Janice's baby pictures. Her childhood if you must. Possibly you would like to take possession?

TONTO

Oh I couldn't …

THERESA

Don't be silly. We still have reams and reams of home movies. Don't we, darling?

LLOYD

Boxes in the basement.

THERESA

See, there you go. Take good care of them. Your child might want to look at them some day.

TONTO and JANICE open up the book.

JANICE

I haven't seen these in years.

TONTO

God you were fat.

LLOYD

Well, if you'll excuse me, I am tempted to try some of that steak and kidney pie right this minute, and wash it down with that pint of Guinness. With that to fortify me, we might actually get the chance to see the play tonight.

THERESA

You never give up, do you?

LLOYD

Not with a pint of Guinness in front of me.

THERESA

You just ate!

LLOYD

Don't bother me with details. If you'll excuse
me ...

LLOYD exits.

THERESA

That man! (*to TONTO*) See what you've done?
He'll be up all night farting. Thanks a lot, Mr.
Hunter.

THERESA exits.

TONTO

Did I do bad?

JANICE

No, you did good. That's just my mother's sense
of humour. She was teasing you. Did you bring
me anything?

TONTO

Just myself.

JANICE

That's all? I seem to have gotten the short end of
the stick.

TONTO

I didn't know if you wanted me to get you
anything. I was just happy to make it inside the
door. I get nervous when white lawyers take a

dislike to me. Especially when I get their daughters pregnant.

JANICE

I phoned Otter Lake today. Barb and Rodney say hello. They want to know when you'll be coming back.

TONTO

That depends on you. Am I going back to the beloved shores of Otter Lake alone, all sad and lonely? I can look pretty pathetic if I have to.

JANICE

More than now?

TONTO

Seriously, Grace. Where do we go from here? Why did you run here instead of to me? I've got nothing against your parents, especially now but Grace, all I want in life is to hold your hand, through both the good and the bad. I know the things you're going through, I've been through a lot of them myself. I can help. When I woke up that morning, and you were gone …

JANICE

I know. I ran again.

TONTO

Running isn't always bad. As long as you're running to something instead of from something. Were you running from the dreams?

JANICE

Yes. They scare me.

TONTO

Why?

JANICE

Because this woman, whom I barely met, is … is … haunting me. Why am I just sitting there, listening to her ramble with me not saying a word?

TONTO

Haven't a clue. They're not my dreams. But there is a reason for these dreams. There has to be. You had to return to Otter Lake to finish your journey. Now you're back here. So where does Anne fit into all of this?

JANICE

I guess she's the mother I never knew.

TONTO

But you met her.

JANICE

Briefly. Too briefly.

TONTO

If you'd known her longer, would things have been different?

JANICE

Oh, I'm sure.

TONTO

How?

JANICE

I could have told her I was sorry for blaming her.
I was sorry for walking out that first time.

TONTO

You did that though. At the grave site. You
poured your heart out. I was there, remember?
That was the beginning of your healing.

JANICE

I asked for forgiveness from Anne ...

TONTO

But not from yourself.

JANICE

The only time I met Anne, on that winter
afternoon, I remember getting up to leave,
leaving her behind like I was rejecting her, she
hugged me good-bye, and ... and ... I accepted it,
but I didn't hug her back. I should've but I
didn't ... I wish I'd hugged the stuffing out of
her.

TONTO

So one home is giving you problems, why not go
to the other home? What does this all mean,
Grace?

JANICE

I told you I don't know.

TONTO
You sure?

Beat.

JANICE
She knew I was pregnant.

TONTO
Who did?

JANICE
Anne. I took the pregnancy test just after the
dreams started. Tonto, she knew before I did.
That was what freaked me out.

TONTO
There are things and beings in the world that
know more than we ever will. But they give us
signs, clues, all around us. We just have to find
them. One of our oldest teachings is that life is a
circle. There is no sunset without a sunrise, no
death without a birth. Anne is talking to you.
About what? What is she here to complete? What
do you need to complete? What is ...

JANICE
I don't know.

TONTO
Grace, you were one of the most important
things to Anne. The day you came back to her, I
don't think seeing Christ himself would have
made her a happier woman.

JANICE

To me, she seemed so calm. It was like she was
afraid to get excited, like it might frighten me
off. Except when …

TONTO

When what?

JANICE

She … she wanted to know if she was a
grandmother. She asked if I had any children.
She said she always wanted to be a grandmother.
She had this glow in her eyes. Now she is a
grandmother. She should be here, with my other
mother.

TONTO

This is how you bring them together.
Grandmothers, mother, child. Three circles of
the Medicine Wheel, all in you. There's no need
for forgiveness here. You have it already, or Anne
wouldn't be there paying you these little visits.
Maybe she's giving you that chance to hug her
back. Maybe she thinks you've got to start
practicing your hugs for the little one. Next time
you see her, say hello for me. Tell her she is
remembered.

TONTO touches her belly.

Wow, I can almost feel the baby already. You're
gonna be huge.

JANICE

I will not be. The mother of this child has been insulted. I demand satisfaction.

TONTO

You and every other woman I've ever dated.

JANICE

How long do you think I'll dream of Anne?

TONTO

That depends on how lucky you are. I have a feeling she'll always be there when you need her.

JANICE goes to hug TONTO but pulls back.

JANICE

Oh you're wet.

TONTO

You just noticed that?

JANICE

Stay here. I'll go see if I can find some of Marshall's old clothes. I'll be right back.

JANICE exits. TONTO finds a family picture of the Wirths. He picks it up and studies it for a moment. Then THERESA enters.

THERESA

That was taken seven years ago. Doesn't she look beautiful?

TONTO
My God yes. You raised a hell of a child, Mrs.
Wirth.

THERESA
Theresa. Welcome to the family.

TONTO
No. Welcome to our family.

They shake hands.

Scene Six

*By this point, ANNE is sitting directly beside the
immobile JANICE. They are a scant few inches from
each other.*

ANNE

For such a small girl you used an awful lot of
diapers. So, one cool fall day while you were
sleeping soundly, I was outside hanging up the
laundry, moving fast to stay warm. That's when I
first noticed the car approaching. It was one of
the newer models, still shiny and clean, so
immediately I knew it wasn't from around here.
A white lady got out, in a grey dress. She didn't
look happy. In fact, she looked kind of grey
herself. She introduced herself as being from the
Children's Aid Society and demanded to see my
daughter. Well, not wanting to cause trouble, I
invited her inside my house. I always had a clean
and tidy house. So after removing my shoes, I led
her to your crib. You were wide awake and
smiling by now, your arms reaching right up to
me. I bundled you into my arms. Then, this
woman said that the Indian Agent told them that
I'd been abandoned by my husband. That I was
alone raising a baby. She said my home wasn't
suitable for a young child. My home wasn't
"suitable"! It hit my heart what she was saying.
She carried you out of our home. I wanted to tell
her about Frank being in the army, how much he
loved us, but I couldn't. I never forgave myself

for that. I had made a promise and I always kept my word. She grabbed you right out of my arms and took you out of our home. I can remember so clearly, you crying and crying, her not doing a thing to calm you. She got in the car, strapped you in the seat beside her, closed the door, and locked it. I tried to get you back. I pulled and pulled on the door but it wouldn't budge. You reached out to me, wanting me but there was nothing I could do. She started the car and drove off with you, like it was nothing. I stood there, watching my baby disappear down the driveway. The sound of you crying was the last thing I heard. I don't know how long I stood there, barefoot. I can still feel the dead leaves and twigs under my feet. That is why I have never walked outside barefoot since. I waited thirty-five long years before I could get the chance tell you how much I loved you. They took you out of my life but never out of my heart. Baby, you're my baby Grace.

ANNE starts to cry. JANICE too. JANICE manages to find the strength to go to ANNE, finally embraces her, and hugs the stuffing out of her.

JANICE
Oh Momma ...

Lights go down.

End.